THE AMAZING WORLD OF GUMBALL

GUMBALL'S SUMMER JOURNAL

that he definitely finished all on his own

by Eric Luper

illustrated by Stephen Reed

CARTOON NETWORK BOOKS

AN IMPRINT OF PENGUIN RANDOM HOUSE

CARTOON NETWORK BOOKS
Penguin Young Readers Group
An Imprint of Penguin Random House LLC

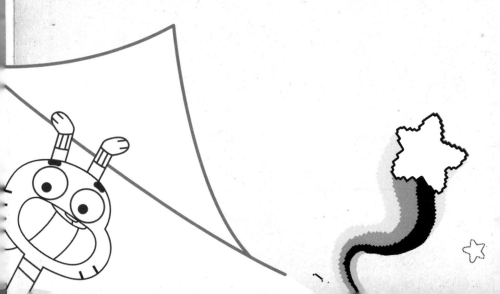

Penguin supports copyright. Copyright fuels creativity, encourages diverse voices, promotes free speech, and creates a vibrant culture. Thank you for buying an authorized edition of this book and for complying with copyright laws by not reproducing, scanning, or distributing any part of it in any form without permission. You are supporting writers and allowing Penguin to continue to publish books for every reader.

™ and © Turner Broadcasting System Europe Limited, Cartoon Network. (s15). All Rights Reserved. Published in 2015 by Cartoon Network Books, an imprint of Penguin Random House LLC, 345 Hudson Street, New York, New York 10014. Printed in the USA.

ISBN 978-0-8431-8282-8   10 9 8 7 6 5 4 3 2 1

Assignment: Summer Journal
Teacher: Miss Simian

Your assignment is to keep a daily summer journal. There are some writing prompts you are required to follow, and I suppose you should use the other blank pages to write about whatever your tiny brain finds interesting. As this is a school project, having any sort of fun is strictly prohibited. This journal is due on the first day of school in September.

In the event you do not complete this journal (Gumball, please pay close attention), you will have detention every day for three months!

I DIDN'T DO MY SUMMER JOURNAL!

9

IF I FIND OUT THAT ANYONE—AND I MEAN **ANYONE**—HAS HELPED GUMBALL WITH HIS JOURNAL, IT'LL MEAN THREE LONG MONTHS OF DETENTION FOR YOU, TOO!

PSST! DON'T LISTEN TO HER! I'LL THINK OF SOME STUFF TO WRITE ABOUT, AND YOU JUST HAVE TO HELP ME WRITE IT. OKAY? IT'S NOT EVEN REALLY CHEATING—IT'S COLLABORATING. AND I KNOW THAT COLLABORATING IS A GOOD THING, BECAUSE I ONCE HEARD MY MOM SAY SO.

YOU KNOW THAT'S NOT THE KIND OF THING I WAS TALKING ABOUT, GUMBALL!

MOM! GO AWAY, I'M DOING MY HOMEWORK!

OKAY, I THINK SHE'S GONE. LET'S GET THIS JOURNAL STARTED!

THINK, GUMBALL, **THINK!** WHAT COULD SOMEONE WRITE ABOUT IN A SUMMER JOURNAL . . . OH, I KNOW!

DARWIN AND I ONCE DECIDED TO WEAR AWESOME KARATE UNIFORMS TO SCHOOL. WHAT IS THE CRAZIEST COSTUME YOU'D WEAR TO SCHOOL?

Head:_____

Neck:_____

Torso:_____

Hands:_____

Lower body:_____

Feet:_____

DRAW YOUR COSTUME BELOW.

WE HAVE THIS, UH, FRIEND AT SCHOOL NAMED TINA REX. IF YOU WERE FRIENDS WITH A T. REX, WHAT WOULD YOU DO?

Summer is a great time to build your very own clubhouse. Draw the floor plan of your dream clubhouse. Spare no expense!

DON'T FORGET THE FOOT-MASSAGE STATION!

DARWIN AND I REALLY LIKE SUPERHEROES. DECK OUT DARWIN WITH EVERY SUPERPOWER YOU CAN THINK OF BY DRAWING THEM ON HIM. LABEL THE POWERS.

Give him a catchy catchphrase:

CONNECT THE DOTS TO DRAW A MAZE FROM START TO FINISH. MAKE IT AS SUPER-TRICKY AS YOU CAN!

START

FINISH

If you had **$10** million, but you had to spend every penny in less than a month, what would you buy? (No hiding money or you **LOSE IT ALL!**)

$10,000,000.00

ITEM	PRICE
―――――――	―――――――
―――――――	―――――――
―――――――	―――――――
―――――――	―――――――
―――――――	―――――――
―――――――	―――――――
―――――――	―――――――
―――――――	―――――――
―――――――	―――――――

ITEM   PRICE

WOW, I REALLY HAVE A LOT OF GRIPES. LIST SOME OF YOUR WORST GRIPES.

1. _____

2. _____

3. _____

4. _____

5. _____

6. _____

7. _____

8. _____

9. _____

10. _____

IT SEEMS YOU ARE ENJOYING YOURSELF TOO MUCH, GUMBALL. ADD UP THE NUMBERS FROM ONE TO A HUNDRED, AND TELL ME THE ANSWER OR YOU'LL BE LICKING THE ERASERS CLEAN.

WAIT, I KNOW THIS!

IF 1 + 100 = 101, AND 2 + 99 = 101, AND 3 + 98 = 101, AND YOU CAN DO THAT ALL THE WAY UP TO 50 + 51 = 101, THEN THE SUM OF EVERY NUMBER FROM 1 TO 100 MUST BE 101 X 50!

WHICH IS . . . UH . . . OKAY, I NEED SOME HELP AGAIN.

WHEW, THAT WAS CLOSE!

I WANT TO HEAR MORE ABOUT THIS PERSON WHO'S DOING YOUR JOURNAL FOR YOU, GUMBALL.

WRITE ABOUT A TIME **YOU** WERE REALLY ANGRY ABOUT SOMETHING. WHAT DID YOU DO ABOUT IT?

NO! YOU CAN'T WRITE ABOUT YOURSELF IN THIS JOURNAL. IT HAS TO BE ALL ABOUT ME!

Summer can be a time when people get on your nerves. Name ways that people you know get on your nerves.

1. _ _ _ _ _ _ _ _ _ _ _ _

2. _ _ _ _ _ _ _ _ _ _ _ _

3. _ _ _ _ _ _ _ _ _ _ _ _

4. _ _ _ _ _ _ _ _ _ _ _ _

5. _ _ _ _ _ _ _ _ _ _ _ _

6. _ _ _ _ _ _ _ _ _ _ _ _

7. _ _ _ _ _ _ _ _ _ _ _ _

8. _ _ _ _ _ _ _ _ _ _ _ _

9. _ _ _ _ _ _ _ _ _ _ _ _

10. _ _ _ _ _ _ _ _ _ _ _

11. _ _ _ _ _ _ _ _ _ _ _

12. _ _ _ _ _ _ _ _ _ _ _

I HEAR THAT MUSTACHES ARE VERY POPULAR THESE DAYS. DRAW CRAZY FACIAL HAIR ON MY FELLOW RESIDENTS OF ELMORE. (OBVIOUSLY MY FACIAL HAIR SHOULD LOOK THE BEST.)

Write about the best summer vacation you can possibly imagine. The sky's the limit!

MY DREAM SUMMER VACATION WOULD BE A WEEK AT A RESORT ON THE RIVER STYX. MMMM . . . ECTOPLASM FRAPPÉS.

Come up with cool code names for you and all your friends using the key below.

First name: The first letter of your first name (take from list 1).

Last name: The last letter of your first name (take from list 2).

Nickname: The first letter of your last name (take from list 3).

	LIST 1	LIST 2	LIST 3
A to C	Hammerhead	McGoo	the Unsinkable
D to F	Slippery	Rockefeller	the Bearhugger
G to I	Lightning	Churchill	the Snake Charmer
J to L	Kickball	Armstrong	the Conquistador
M to O	Lead-Fist	Mooney	the Cave Dweller
P to R	Treestump	Rodriguez	the Stormbringer
S to U	Stinkbug	Iron-Jaw	the Tank Crusher
V to Z	Xerxes	Lumberyard	the Candy Eater

WAIT A SECOND. I'M SLIPPERY MOONEY THE CANDY EATER? AWESOME!

GUMBALL, THESE CODE NAMES DON'T SEEM TO MATCH ANY OF YOUR SO-CALLED "FRIENDS" HERE AT ELMORE! ARE YOU GETTING HELP WITH YOUR JOURNAL?

THEY'RE MY FRIENDS FROM MY EXTRACURRICULAR CLUBS AND SPORTS HOBBIES, MISS SIMIAN.

Write about a time you felt scared. Try to describe the situation and what you did to feel better.

- -

- -

- -

- -

- -

- -

- -

- -

- -

- - - - - - - - - - - - - - - - - - - -

- - - - - - - - - - - - - - - - - -

- - - - - - - - - - - - - - - - -

- - - - - - - - - - - - - - - -

- - - - - - - - - - - - - - -

I'M AFRAID OF SHARP OBJECTS. THEY MAKE ME FEEL VERY POPPY!

ONE TIME, MY PARENTS GAVE ME A CELL PHONE, BUT IT WAS ONE OF THOSE OLD BRICK-SIZE MODELS THAT DIDN'T HAVE ANY GAMES ON IT OR ANYTHING. WRITE A JOURNAL ENTRY FROM MY POINT OF VIEW DESCRIBING MY EXCITEMENT . . . AND MY DISAPPOINTMENT. I'LL EVEN HELP GET YOU STARTED. AHEM!

Oh man, I can't wait until I get home today. Mom said I'm

finally mature enough to get a cell phone!

_____

_____

_____

_____

_____

ANY STUDENT CAUGHT USING A CELL PHONE DURING THE SCHOOL DAY WILL BE SENT TO MR. SMALL'S OFFICE!

I LONG TO ENRICH YOUR MIND WITH POEMS OF PEACE.

If you could be the best in the world at five things, what would they be?

I'M AWESOME AT EVERYTHING!

1. _____

_____

2. _____

_____

3. _____

_____

4. _____

_____

5. _____

_____

ONE TIME, DARWIN, ANAIS, DAD, AND I MADE MOM SO ANGRY THAT SHE TURNED INTO A CRAZY MONSTER. WHAT ARE A FEW THINGS YOU'VE DONE TO MAKE SOMEONE MAD?

IT WOULD BE BEST IF YOU TURNED AROUND AND RAN RIGHT NOW . . .

1. _____

2. _____

3. _____

4. _____

5. _____

6. _____

7. _____

This summer, try to join a club! What are the five coolest clubs you can imagine?

1. _____

2. _____

3. _____

4. _____

5. _____

FEELINGS OF INCLUSION ARE IMPORTANT TO EVERY CHILD'S HEALTHY DEVELOPMENT.

I CAN'T FIND A SINGLE CLUB THAT WILL HAVE ME. EXCEPT THE REJECT CLUB. SIGH.

CHOPPED LIVER AND GARLIC CLUB!

THERE IS NO WAY THESE CLUBS WILL BE ALLOWED AT ELMORE JUNIOR HIGH. DETENTION FOR YOU FOR THINKING OUTSIDE OF THE BOX.

Summertime is video-game time! If you could create your own video game, what would it be like?

Title: _____

Where does the story take place?

_____

Who is the main character?

_____

What is he/she trying to do?_____

_____

Does the hero have any special powers, abilities, or gear?

_____

Describe the final scene. _____

I THINK *TOASTER WARS* WOULD BE AN EXCELLENT GAME.

GUMBALL'S AND MY FAVORITE VIDEO GAME IS THE *TALE OF ZELMORE*.

OH, I KNOW A GOOD JOURNAL ACTIVITY!
WOULD YOU RATHER . . .

Be super rich   or   Live twice as long?

Get a two-week dream vacation alone   or   Spend a day at home with anyone?

Be a vampire   or   Be a werewolf?

Never eat candy again   or   Never play video games again?

Be a wizard   or   Be a ninja?

Have a private boat   or   Have a private helicopter?

Eat a bowl of worms   or   Eat only brussels sprouts for a year?

I'D RATHER YOU GET BACK TO WORK ON YOUR JOURNAL THAN WASTE TIME ON QUESTIONS LIKE THESE!

DARWIN AND I MANAGE TO GET EXCUSED FROM GYM CLASS EVERY DAY. WE ARE KIND OF GENIUSES WHEN IT COMES TO EXCUSES. MAKE UP THE CRAZIEST EXCUSE TO GET YOU OUT OF GYM CLASS.

EVERYTHING YOU LEARN IN GYM CLASS WILL BE USEFUL SOMEDAY!

IT'S NOT SWEAT; IT'S MY ORGANS CRYING.

COACH TOLD ME TO CUT OUT CARBS, BUT THAT'S ALL I AM!

I LOVE THE SMELL OF DESPAIR ON A MONDAY MORNING. AND NOTHING BRINGS OUT THE STENCH OF DESPAIR LIKE A HEALTHY DOSE OF GYM CLASS!

CAN YOU FILL IN THESE BLANK PARTS FOR ME? I'M GOING TO GO BATHE IN SOME AFTERSHAVE.

Once upon a time, Gumball, Darwin, and Anais were sitting on the couch in (the) _____ while their

<a place>

parents were at the school parents' evening.

"I'm going upstairs," Anais said.

"No!" Gumball cried. "Don't you know that 79 percent of

_____ accidents happen on the stairs?

<noun>

You are safer here, sitting on the _____

<noun>

and _____ TV."

<verb ending in "ing">

Anais sighed. "O-kaaay."

Anais sat down on the couch to watch an episode of *Daisy*

_____. Suddenly, Gumball and Darwin

<animal>

started hitting the TV with baseball _____!

<plural noun>

"Are you completely out of your minds?" Anais asked.

"Commercials! They'll corrupt your

_____!" Gumball replied. "It was the

<part of the body>

responsible thing to do."

"How could Mom put you in charge?" Anais

grumbled. Then she opened her book and started

_____ it.

<verb ending in "ing">

Darwin snatched the _____ out of

<noun>

Anais's hands.

"What is wrong with you?" Anais _____.

<verb (past tense)>

"Paper cuts," Darwin responded.

"Ridiculous," Anais said. "And look at the mess you're

making."

"It's a small _____ to pay for your safety,

<noun>

Anais," Gumball said _____.

<adverb>

"Excuse me," Anais replied, "but who makes your

breakfast every _____? And who helps

<noun>

you with your math _____?"

<noun>

"You, of course!"

"Exactly. So I should be in charge."

"But Mom put *us* in charge," Gumball said.

Anais folded her _____ and scowled.

<part of the body (plural)>

"I know what will cheer you up!" Darwin exclaimed. "Let's

go for a walk in (the) _____."

<a place>

"Fine," Anais replied, sighing.

Gumball and Darwin really wanted to act

_____ and keep Anais safe, so they knew
<adverb>

it would be best if she wore a leash.

Then, Gumball decided that Anais must be hungry.

They gave her a big plate of _____, but
<noun>

Darwin suddenly realized she could choke on it! So they

_____ up her food for her and spat it back
<verb (past tense)>

onto her plate.

Anais was just about to tell her brothers exactly how

_____ they were being, but then Mrs.
<adjective>

Watterson came home . . .

HEH-HEH, YOU DON'T WANT TO HEAR WHAT MOM SAID
WHEN SHE GOT HOME. LET'S MOVE ON TO SOMETHING ELSE.

HOW ABOUT DOING THIS WORD SEARCH?
WORD SEARCHES ARE WAY MORE FUN THAN
WORKING ON BORING STORIES ABOUT HOW
RESPONSIBLE DARWIN AND I ARE!

F O C H O H A D I A
O R G E S A R A H N
T C H E C T O R A A
B L E S L I E W C I
O A U T T O B I A S
P Y T I A L A N R N
E T A R B O B E R T
N O T N A T E R I E
N N X T I N A R E X
Y B A N A N A J O E

ALAN, ANAIS, ANTON, BANANA JOE, BOBERT, CARRIE, CLAYTON, DARWIN, HECTOR, IDAHO, LESLIE, OCHO, PENNY, SARAH, TERI, TINA REX, TOBIAS

SPECIAL BONUS: PUT THE LEFTOVER LETTERS TOGETHER TO SPELL OUT A SUPER-SECRET MESSAGE!

_ _ _ _ _ _ _ _ _ _ _ _ _ _ _ _ _ _ _ _

_ _ _ _ _ _ _ _ _ _ _ _ _ _ _ _ _ _ _ _

_ _ _ _ _ _ _ _ _ _ _ _ _ _ _ _ _ _ _ _

MAZE TIME! HELP ME NAVIGATE THE STREETS OF ELMORE WITHOUT RUNNING INTO ANY UNSAVORY CHARACTERS WHO MIGHT DELAY ME.

IT'S ALWAYS GOOD TO HAVE AN EXCUSE HANDY. HELP ME FIGURE OUT AN EXCUSE I CAN USE FOR EACH PERSON I MIGHT RUN INTO.

Miss Simian (knows I forgot my homework):

_____

Tina Rex (wants to go to the dance with me):

_____

Sarah (wants my e-mail address):

_____

Mrs. Watterson (wants me to rake the lawn):

_____

Banana Joe (wants to come over to play video games):

_____

BACK, AND IT'S ALWAYS GOOD TO PRACTICE YOUR AIM. HOLD YOUR PENCIL HIGH ABOVE THE BOOK AND SEE HOW MANY TIMES IN A ROW YOU CAN HIT HER WHEN YOU DROP IT.

ALL THE BEST ACTION MOVIES COME OUT OVER THE SUMMER. IF YOU COULD CREATE YOUR OWN ACTION MOVIE, WHAT WOULD IT BE LIKE?

Title: _____

Main character:

_____

Skills/powers:

_____

Place/setting:

_____

Bad guys along the way:

_____

Final boss:

_____

Mega-happy ending:

_____

DRAW A PICTURE OF YOUR ACTION-MOVIE HERO BELOW.

GUMBALL AND I ONCE MADE A MOVIE CALLED *NINJA GEORGE*. NINJA GEORGE MET AN OGRE, A DRAGON, AND A BEAUTIFUL WOMAN, AND HE DEFEATED THEM ALL! THEN HE HAD TO FIGHT THE COLONEL, AND THERE WAS A MEGA-HAPPY ENDING.

Have you ever had to do something that made you nervous? Describe what happened and how you got through it.

OH MAN. CAN'T SOMEONE ASK PENNY ON A DATE FOR ME? MAYBE I SHOULD TRICK HER, SO SHE DOESN'T EVEN KNOW IT'S A DATE . . .

HEY! CAN YOU THINK OF A MEGA-EXCELLENT WAY FOR ME TO ASK PENNY TO DO SOMETHING ALONE WITHOUT HER REALIZING IT'S ACTUALLY A DATE?

JUST BECAUSE IT MAKES YOU NERVOUS DOESN'T MEAN YOU CAN'T DO IT. *SIGH* . . .

ENOUGH FUN AND GAMES. TIME TO GET SOME SERIOUS JOURNALING DONE! WRITE ABOUT WHAT YOU DO WHEN YOU ARE OUTSIDE MY CONTROL.

WOULDN'T YOU RATHER PLAY VIDEO GAMES THAN WRITE IN A JOURNAL?

LET YOUR DREAMS
FLOAT FREE!

BE SURE TO KEEP YOUR JOURNAL AWAY FROM WATER OR IT'LL GET SOGGY.

WRITE ABOUT
NICE THINGS!

DON'T FORGET TO ADD HOW THINGS MAKE YOU FEEL ... LIKE OBSESSIVE LOVE!

WE WATTERSONS LOVE TO DRESS UP FOR HALLOWEEN. DRAW A COSTUME ON EVERYONE IN MY FAMILY. THE CRAZIER THE BETTER!

Write a sentence using words that all start with the same letter. Make your sentence as long as you can!

THAT'S GOING TO BE EXTREMELY DIFFICULT. PREPOSITIONS AND ARTICLES SHOULDN'T COUNT.

PREPO . . . ARTIES . . . WHAT?

PREPOSITIONS ARE WORDS LIKE *IN*, *ABOVE*, AND *BESIDE*. ARTICLES INCLUDE *A*, *AN*, *THE*, AND SO ON.

EXACTLY—THAT'S WHAT I SAID!

YOU SHOULD CHALLENGE YOUR FRIENDS TO SAY THE SENTENCE AS QUICKLY AS THEY CAN. THAT WOULD BE HI-**LAR**-IOUS.

SASSY SUSSIE SUPPOSEDLY SUSTAINED SALMONELLA SLIDING ACROSS SIXTEEN SLOPPY, STINKY SALMON-SOAKED SALAD STATIONS.

Color the next page any color you want. Then describe a scene made up of as many things that color as possible.

WHAT ARE YOU DOING? THIS IS NO JOURNAL! YOU'RE JUST PLAYING SILLY GAMES.

GAMES ARE A SPLENDID WAY TO LEARN!

AS LONG AS YOU'RE NOT PLAYING "SHE LOVES ME; SHE LOVES ME NOT"!

WRITE A HAIKU. IT SHOULD HAVE FIVE SYLLABLES IN THE FIRST AND LAST LINES, AND THE MIDDLE LINE SHOULD HAVE SEVEN SYLLABLES.

_ _ _ _ _ _ _ _ _ _ _ _

_ _ _ _ _ _ _ _ _ _ _ _ _ _ _ _

_ _ _ _ _ _ _ _ _ _ _ _

COMPLEX BANANAS. IF YOU PEEL ME, DO I NOT SHOW YOU MY SOFT SIDE?

Summer is a great time to finally do some exercise. See how many of the following exercises you and your friends can do in sixty seconds.

Sit-ups ___

Push-ups ___

Windmills ___

Jumping Jacks ___

Ninja kicks ___

THINK OF PUSH-UPS NOT AS PUSHING YOUR BODY UP, BUT AS PUSHING THE EARTH DOWN.

PUSH-UPS ARE EASY FOR ME.

UGH, EXERCISE. EVEN THE WORD SOUNDS TIRING!

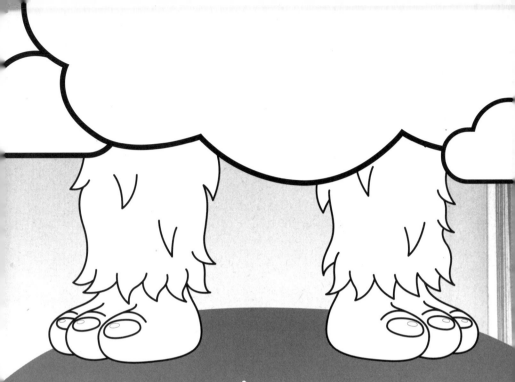

HEY, HAVE I MENTIONED HECTOR YET?
HECTOR IS MY FRIEND. HE'S, LIKE, A
HUNDRED FEET TALL. WHAT WOULD YOU DO
IF YOU HAD A HUNDRED-FOOT FRIEND?

_____

_____

_____

_____

_____

_____

Figure out which number each child represents by using the total values at the end of each row and column.

😊	😊	😊	🐰	**15**
🐰	😊	😊	😊	**14**
😊	😊	🐰	😊	**16**
🐰	🐰	🐰	🐰	**20**
17	**15**	**16**	**17**	

😊 = ?   😊 = ?   🐰 = ?

_____   _____   _____

JOLLY GOOD! A BIT OF A MATH EXERCISE FOR SUMMER HOLIDAY. HOW FUN!

NO CHILD HAS ANY VALUE.

ENTER IF YOU DARE!
BUT PLEASE KNOCK FIRST. AND KNOCK LIGHTLY SO YOU DON'T STARTLE US.

DEFACING SCHOOL PROPERTY? THERE ARE DIRE CONSEQUENCES FOR CUTTING PAGES OUT OF A JOURNAL!

GUMBALL, ARE YOU STILL COMING TO MY PARTY?

PENNY! MY DATE! DARWIN, TURN OUT THOSE FLASHLIGHTS. I'VE GOTTA GO!

How much do you know about your best friend? Take this test to find out:

Favorite color?_____

Favorite food?_____

Middle name?_____

Favorite TV show?_____

Favorite song?_____

Favorite movie?_____

Favorite season?_____

Birthday?_____

Favorite game?_____

Favorite book?_____

HAS YOUR BEST FRIEND EVER:

Traveled out of the country?   **Y/n**

Gone on an upside-down roller coaster?   **Y/n**

Won a trophy?   **Y/n**

Broken a bone?   **Y/n**

Been in the ocean?   **Y/n**

Eaten sushi?   **Y/n**

Most students become very excited before the summer break. List five things you've ever been super-excited for.

1. _____

_____

2. _____

_____

3. _____

_____

4. _____

_____

5. _____

_____

I ONCE UNCOVERED A SECRET THAT I WAS SURE WOULD LEAD TO OUR HIDDEN FAMILY TREASURE. I WAS SO EXCITED!

JOYFUL BURGER

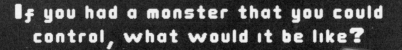

If you had a monster that you could control, what would it be like?

HEY, GUMBALL? REMEMBER THAT TIME WE CREATED A GOOPY MONSTER IN THE MICROWAVE?

OH YEAH! BOY, WAS THAT A DISASTER. IT ENDED UP EATING EVERYONE IN OUR FAMILY, ALONG WITH MUCH OF THE REST OF ELMORE.

Elmore Junior High has a lot of interesting students. There is a ghost, a cloud, a piece of toast, a banana, a T. rex, and who knows what else. Pick an item from the list below, and imagine you go to school with him or her. Draw the character, and describe what that person would be like.

beach ball   ——————————————————————

chair   ——————————————————————

ice cube   ——————————————————————

owl   ——————————————————————

coffee mug   ——————————————————————

rainbow   ————————————

pillow   ————————————

scissors   ——————————————————————

campfire   ——————————————————————

THERE ARE MORE DIFFERENT STUDENTS HERE NOW THAN I'VE SEEN IN THREE HUNDRED THOUSAND YEARS!

HEY . . . WHY WASN'T I LISTED? I'M A BLUE CAT!

YOU? WHAT ABOUT ME? I AM A FISH. WITH **LEGS**!

91

QUICK! LIST THREE PLACES IN THE WORLD YOU'D LOVE TO VISIT!

1. _____

2. _____

3. _____

IT'S STRANGE THAT SOME OF THESE ENTRIES CLEARLY HAVE NOTHING TO DO WITH YOU OR ANYTHING AT ELMORE JUNIOR HIGH, GUMBALL.

IT JUST GOES TO SHOW YOU THE DEPTH OF MY KNOWLEDGE AND CREATIVITY, MISS SIMIAN.

IF YOU COULD BE THE BEST ATHLETE IN THE WORLD IN ANY SPORT, WHICH SPORT WOULD IT BE, AND WHY?

If you could have any billboard posted on your local highway, what would it say? Draw it below.

ONCE, I DEFACED A BILLBOARD JUST TO SHOW MR. FITZGERALD THAT I WANTED TO BE HIS FRIEND.

Some students like to go on adventures over the summer. What is the most incredible adventure you've ever had? Write about it below.

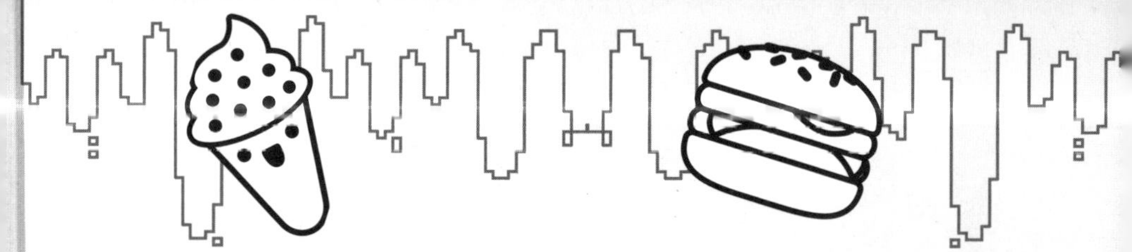

What are your five favorite foods?

1. _____

2. _____

3. _____

4. _____

5. _____

DUDE, FOOD RULES.

YOU LIKE ICE CREAM, DON'T YOU, GUMBALL?

What is your least favorite food?

_____

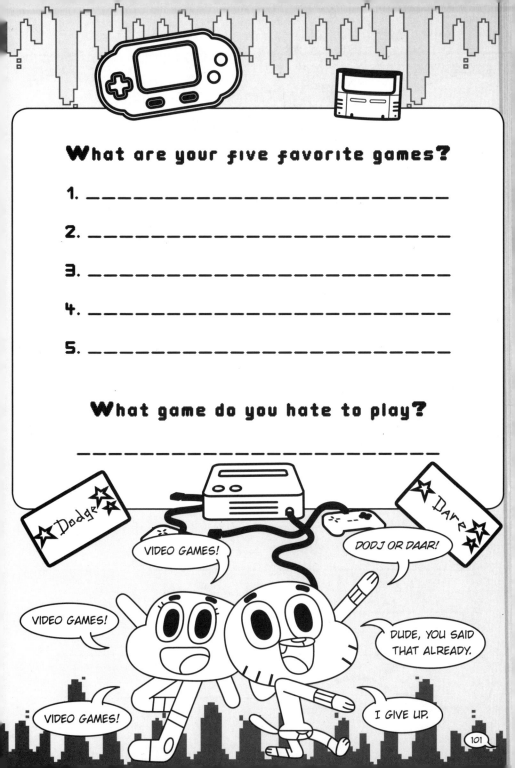

What are your five favorite games?

1. _____

2. _____

3. _____

4. _____

5. _____

What game do you hate to play?

_____

VIDEO GAMES!

DODJ OR DAAR!

VIDEO GAMES!

DUDE, YOU SAID THAT ALREADY.

VIDEO GAMES!

I GIVE UP.

LIKE THAT TIME I GOT SUPER-ANGRY AT DARWIN OVER A DREAM I HAD. THAT WAS BAD. REALLY BAD.

GUMBALL MAY NEED SOME HELP WITH THIS ONE. HOLD YOUR PEN STRAIGHT OUT AT ARM'S LENGTH, DROP IT TEN TIMES, AND COUNT THE NUMBER OF TIMES YOU HIT TOBIAS.

Scoring:

0 = What, are you blind or something?

1 = Pathetic.

2 = One better than pathetic.

3 = Shaky hands!

4 = Tobias is starting to feel something.

5 = Not bad.

6 = Fin-flapping-tastic!

7 = Tobias is in deep, deep trouble!

8 = With a little more practice, you could go pro.

9 = You are a pencil-dropping machine!

10 = Perfecto!

11 = CHEATER!

WOO-HOO, I'VE FINISHED MY JOURNAL!

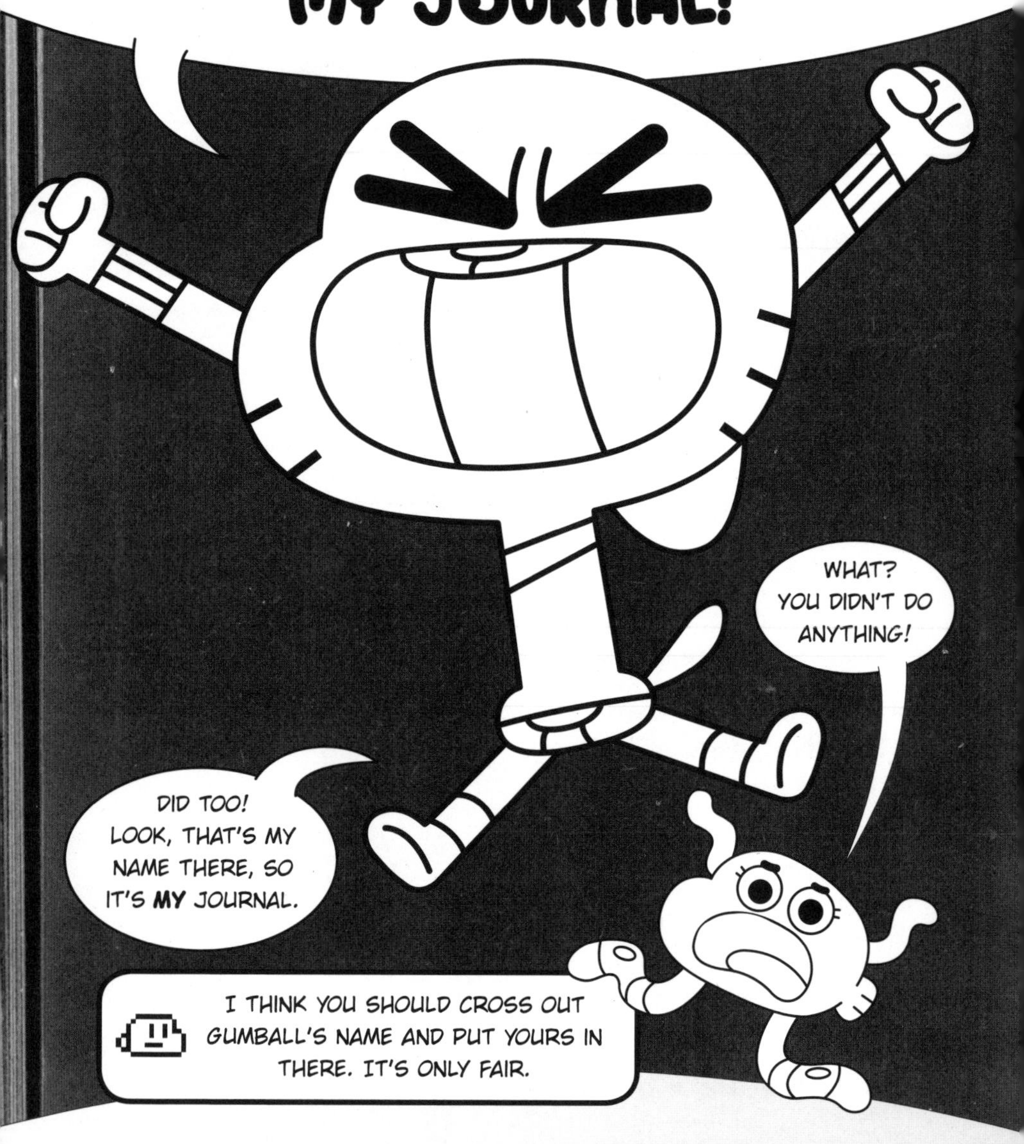

-UM ALL WATT N

Dear Principal Brown,

I regret to inform you that I will have to miss the next three months of school. I have contracted a rare disease called Blue Cat Fever, which requires me to undergo intense care and rehabilitation in the deepest area of the Congo. I should state that this in no way has to do with Gumball's recent three-month detention. I'd appreciate your cooperation in this matter and look forward to my healthy return. (We are still on for our secret date next week, though, right?)

Very truly yours,

Miss Simian